The Great Bake-off

by Steven Otfinoski
illustrated by Paul Yalowitz

CHARACTERS:

NARRATOR

MANUEL

JUANITA

LUÍS

JENNA

SHAWN

JENNA'S DAD

BINGO, JENNA'S DOG

LADY WITH DOG

MODERN CURRICULUM PRESS
Pearson Learning Group

NARRATOR: Here come fifth-graders Manuel, Juanita, Luís, Jenna, and Shawn. They're on their way home from school.

MANUEL: I can't believe it. We still don't have enough money for our class trip to Wacky World Amusement Park!

JUANITA: We tried, Manuel. Think of all the fund-raising activities our class has done so far this year.

LUÍS: You mean the car wash that raised three dollars?

JENNA: It wasn't our fault that it rained.

JUANITA: Okay, so the car wash was a washout. And so was the backyard circus, thanks to Luís and his sheepdog!

JENNA: We told you your dog would make a lousy elephant!

LUÍS: He was great until his fake ears fell off!

MANUEL: Look, arguing won't do any good. We've got to think of something new. There are still a few weeks left before we are supposed to go on the class trip.

JUANITA: Manuel's right. We just have to come up with a surefire way to raise the money we need.

LUÍS: I know! Let's have a bake sale. The PTA always makes tons of money with their bake sales.

SHAWN: Say, that's a great idea! We'll get our parents to bake cakes and pastries and we'll sell them at school!

JUANITA: Don't count on my dad. He hates to bake.

MANUEL: My mom never has the time. She works long hours.

LUÍS: How about your mom and dad, Jenna? Don't you have two stoves in your kitchen because they cook so much?

JENNA: We do. But they don't have as much time to cook anymore. Not since Dad started his second job at the Kitty Boutique.

LUÍS: Well, *scratch* that idea.

SHAWN: Ha!

MANUEL: Wait a minute. Why can't *we* do the baking?

JUANITA: Are you serious?

MANUEL: I've watched my mom bake plenty of times. It's no big deal. All you have to do is open a cookbook and follow the recipes.

JUANITA: That might be fun. We could bake bread and cakes and lots of gooey pastries.

SHAWN: And don't forget some peanut butter cookies! They're my favorite!

JUANITA: Those too! I bet in one day we could bake everything we'd need for the sale!

JENNA: We can use our kitchen. It will go faster with two stoves. My mom will be running errands on Saturday, and my dad will be working at home all day. So he can help us.

LUÍS: Do you think he'll mind?

JENNA: No, he'll love it. He always says that baking is one of life's pleasures.

MANUEL: Then Saturday it is! We'll meet at Jenna's and bake up a storm!

LUÍS: Now you're cooking!

MANUEL (*to the others*): Just ignore him.

NARRATOR: It's Saturday morning. All the friends are here at Jenna's house. Her dad is home. And here are Luís and Manuel now.

(LUÍS *and* MANUEL *enter, carrying bags of groceries.*)

JENNA'S DAD: Hi, everyone! It's nice to see you. (*He looks at the dog.*) Bingo says hi too.

JENNA: You didn't have to buy all that stuff. We have everything here in the kitchen.

LUÍS: You can never have enough flour and eggs when you're baking.

SHAWN: Well, let's get started. What should we make first?

JENNA: How about some bread? Everyone loves homemade bread.

LUÍS: Great idea! The bread will really bring in the *dough*!

JUANITA: Oh, no! That joke is *stale*!

LUÍS (*shrugging*): Sorry, I knew it was *crumb*-y. But I couldn't resist it!

SHAWN: There he goes again. . . .

JENNA'S DAD: I think he's very funny.

JENNA (*opening a cookbook*): Oh, Dad! Well, anyway, here's a recipe for whole-wheat bread. We need water, shortening, eggs, butter, flour, and a package of yeast.

8

MANUEL: Ah, the pleasures of cooking!

JUANITA: I never knew baking could be such fun.

JENNA: We'd better add more of everything. We want to make at least six loaves of bread in this first batch.

LUÍS: Good idea. Six more of everything, including the yeast.

JENNA'S DAD: I'm sure you're joking. Now don't go overboard. You *can* have too much of a good thing.

JENNA (*looking at door, noticing that it was left open a little and that Bingo is about to run out*): Bingo!

NARRATOR: Uh-oh. There goes Bingo . . . right out that open door.

JENNA'S DAD: Come back, Bingo. Now you kids be careful. I'll be right back, as soon as I get Bingo.

ALL THE CHILDREN: We will. Good luck!

SHAWN: Do you want some help?

JENNA'S DAD: No, thanks. You all have a lot of work to do here. Just be careful.

(JENNA'S DAD *runs out the door.*)

SHAWN: I hope he catches Bingo fast. Well, let's get back to baking. What's yeast for, anyway?

JUANITA: Don't you know anything about baking, Shawn? The yeast is what makes the bread rise.

SHAWN: Really? Then let's put in plenty more!

NARRATOR: Well, it looks as if everyone is working hard. The boys are kneading the bread dough. The girls over there are making a cake.

JENNA: This is easy! You just pour in the cake mix, add a few things, and it's ready to bake.

JUANITA: What temperature should the oven be?

JENNA: Hmm. That part of the package has batter all over it. I can't read the temperature. It's either 350 or 550.

JUANITA: Well, which do you think it is?

JENNA: Better go with 550. The cake will bake quicker if the oven's hotter.

JUANITA: Makes sense to me.

NARRATOR: The girls preheat the oven to 550 degrees and then put the cake in.

JUANITA: That's it! Now let's make some cookies while the cake is baking.

SHAWN: Did I hear someone mention cookies?

JENNA: It's Shawn, being himself. Just remember, Shawn, these cookies are for selling, NOT eating.

SHAWN: But someone has to taste test them, right?

JUANITA: Maybe, but let's make them first.

JENNA: The recipe for the cookies is in that folder on the counter.

LUÍS: I'll get it.

NARRATOR (*whispering*): That recipe Luís is taking out of the folder says "Peanut Butter" on it. But just between you and me, it's not for cookies.

JENNA: Okay, Luís. Start reading what we need to make the cookies.

LUÍS (*reading the recipe*): Let's see . . . a cup of butter, a teaspoon of salt. . . .

JENNA: This is a breeze.

NARRATOR: Ten minutes later the cookie batter is made and the cookies are ready for the oven.

JENNA: We'll put them into the oven with the bread. Just remember to take them out in twenty minutes.

JUANITA: I'll set the timer.

SHAWN: Cookies cook up fast. I like that.

MANUEL: Now we just sit and wait while all the goodies bake.

NARRATOR: DING! There goes the timer!

SHAWN: The cookies are ready!

MANUEL: Yum! I can smell the sweet fragrance of peanut butter!

NARRATOR: Jenna inspects the oven and then carefully takes out each cookie sheet with pot holders.

JENNA: Now we have to wait until they cool off before we try one.

SHAWN: Just one?

JUANITA (*grinning*): Shawn, it's too bad your brain isn't as hard-working as your stomach!

SHAWN (*grinning back*): Hey, I'm a growing boy!

NARRATOR: Jenna's dad finally caught Bingo. Here he is with the little dog.

JENNA'S DAD (*entering with the dog in his arms*): I finally caught him. Bingo here gave me quite a chase. Wait a minute. Do you guys smell something burning? (JENNA'S DAD *puts the dog down.*)

LUÍS: Not me.

JUANITA: I do. What *is* that?

JENNA: Maybe there's a fire down the block.

SHAWN: It smells closer than that.

NARRATOR: Don't look now, but something is definitely burning.

JENNA and **JUANITA:** Our cake!

NARRATOR: Jenna's dad takes the cake out of the oven. Manuel fans the back door to let smoke out.

MANUEL: It's burnt to a cinder!

JUANITA: It's ruined!

JENNA: I guess we had the temperature too high.

SHAWN: Well, at least we still have our cookies . . . and all that bread.

LUÍS: I can smell the bread baking. What a yummy fragrance!

JUANITA: Don't you think we should check it and see if it has risen yet?

NARRATOR: Luís is opening the oven door. He inspects the baking bread. He's not going to like what he sees!

LUÍS: Yikes! What happened to our bread?

JENNA: It looks as if it turned into the Blob!

MANUEL: What did we do wrong?

SHAWN: Maybe we used too much flour!

JUANITA: More like too much yeast!

JENNA: The whole kitchen's a mess!

SHAWN: This is depressing. I think I'll try a cookie.

NARRATOR: Uh-oh! Watch Shawn's face when he bites into that thing.

SHAWN (*grimacing*): Yuck! They're terrible!

JENNA: What's the matter with them?

SHAWN: They're hard as a rock!

LUÍS: I wonder what went wrong? We followed the recipe.

JENNA: Let me see that recipe. (*She scans the recipe.*) No wonder they're hard! This is a recipe for peanut butter dog biscuits! Not cookies!

BINGO: Woof-woof!

LUÍS: Oops! This is really (*barking*) RUFF!

(*Everyone glares at him, including the narrator.*)

JUANITA: This is just great. Our big bake sale has turned into a total bust!

MANUEL (*thinking*): I'm not so sure of that.

BINGO: Woof-woof!

JENNA: What do you mean, Manuel?

MANUEL: I mean these dog biscuits have given me a great idea. I think we can still raise the money for our class trip.

SHAWN: So tell us how.

MANUEL: I will. But first let's clean up this kitchen. I'm sure Jenna's dad would appreciate that.

JENNA'S DAD: You got *that* right!

NARRATOR: Welcome to the school pet fair! Jenna and Manuel over there are selling dog biscuits to customers. Shawn is selling birdseed.

MANUEL: These dog biscuits are selling like hotcakes!

JENNA: This was a great idea to have a pet fair, Manuel.

SHAWN: I have to admit it is more unusual than a bake sale, and the pets are enjoying it as much as the people!

LADY WITH DOG: I was told you have a Walk-Your-Dog Service.

JENNA: Yes, ma'am. Just see that fellow over there. He's our dog walker.

LUÍS (*surrounded by dogs*): How did I get stuck with this job?

JUANITA (*surrounded by cats*): Well, you found the dog biscuit recipe. It was the *leash* we could do!

(*Everyone laughs.*)

MANUEL: Just remember, guys! All the money we make will pay for our class trip.

LUÍS: That's right. It just goes to show that sometimes things can work out fine, even when they "go to the dogs!"

(*Everyone groans.*)

(LUÍS *howls and yips like a dog.*)

(*Everyone laughs.*)